Contents

Meet the Mystery Mob

Name:

Gummy

FYI: Gummy hasn't got much brain – and even fewer teeth.

Loves: Soup.

Hates: Toffee chews.

Fact: The brightest thing about him is his shirt.

Name:

Lee

FYI: If Lee was any cooler he'd be a cucumber.

Loves: Hip-hop.

Hates: Hopscotch.

Fact: He has his own designer label (which he peeled off a tin).

Name:

FYI: Rob lives in his own world – he's just visiting planet Earth.

Loves: Daydreaming.

Hates: Nightmares.

Fact: Rob always does his homework – he just forgets to write it down.

Name:

FYI: Dwayne is smarter than a tree full of owls.

Loves: Anything complicated.

Hates: Join-the-dots books.

Fact: If he was any brighter you could use him as a floodlight at football matches.

Name:

Chet

FYI: Chet is as brave as a lion with steel jaws.

Loves: Having adventures.

Hates: Knitting.

Fact: He's as tough as the chicken his granny cooks for his tea.

Name:

Adi

FYI: Adi is as happy as a football fan with tickets to the big match.

Loves: Telling jokes.

Hates: Moaning minnies.

Fact: He knows more jokes than a jumbo joke book.

1

Sweet Things

The Mystery Mob are going on a tour
of the Sweet Sensation Candy factory.
They're looking forward to eating
loads of free sweet samples.

Adi   This place is soooo wicked.

Chet   It smells of sugar and chocolate
           and all sorts of good stuff.

Rob   I can't wait to go on the tour.

Dwayne Right. I want to see
how they make the Jelly Bellies.
They're my favourites.

Adi   Oh, it's easy to make a Jelly Belly
– you just eat tons and tons
of sweets!

Gummy   Adi, I wish you'd eat
a gob stopper. Then we wouldn't
have to listen to your rotten jokes.

Adi   Okay, but you really shouldn't
             eat too many sweets, you know.
             My little brother did,
             and I've got to take him
             to the dentist today.

Rob   Oh no – what time
             do you have to be there?

Adi   Tooth hurty. Two thirty – get it?!

Lee   Doh!

A man in a white coat and hat comes up
to the boys.

Steve   Hi, guys. My name's Steve
              and I'm going to show you round
              the Sweet Sensation factory.

Gummy Cool.

Steve   Right, let's go, but guys,
don't touch or taste anything
unless I say so. Okay?

Mystery Mob

Okay.

But before Steve can take
the Mystery Mob off into the factory,
an alarm sounds. Steve looks worried.

Steve   Sorry, boys, the tour's off.

11

Dwayne Why? What's up?
What does that alarm mean?

Steve It means that millions
of Vanilla Thrillers,
our best selling sweet,
have gone missing – again.

Chet No way! Who's taking them?

Steve A thief called the Candyman.
We don't know who he is
or how he does it. But he's
got to be stopped
before we go bust!

Steve strides away.

Lee   Hey, no way are we going to let
the Candyman ruin our day.
Come on, let's track him down.

The boys split up and go to different parts
of the factory.

Killer Vanilla

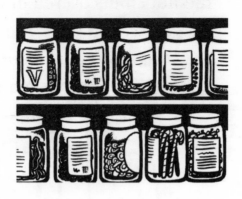

Rob and Lee are standing
next to a bench that has lots of jars
filled with brightly coloured sweets.

Rob   Look, there are millions
of sweets here.

Lee   Yeah, but they're not
Vanilla Thrillers.

Rob   Hey, Lee, what exactly
is a Vanilla Thriller?

Lee   It's only the coolest candy ever.

Rob   All right! Um … but I still
don't know what it is.

Lee   (sighing) It's a tiny bit of
red hot chilli covered in white
chocolate. You put a handful
of Thrillers in your mouth
and they blow your head off!
I call them Killer Vanilla Thrillers.

Rob   Wow, that's sooo wicked!
Er … but I think I'll give them
a miss. Red hot chilli
gives me bottom burps.

Lee   Oh, you're such a total wimp.

Rob   I can't help it. Anyway,
I prefer sticky toffee.

Lee   Right. I guess that explains
why you're a bit stuck up.

Rob   (angrily) I'm not stuck up,
I'm … oh right. I get it. It's a joke.

Lee   Yeah, but the joke'll be on us
if we don't hurry up and find out
who the Candyman is –
and how he steals
the Vanilla Thrillers.

But Rob isn't listening to Lee.

Rob Er, Lee, why is there a ferret in the sweet factory?

Lee Leave it out, Rob. We've finished cracking jokes.

Rob It's no joke. There's a flipping great ferret sitting on that table. It's got a bag of Vanilla Thrillers in its mouth!

Lee You're kidding me.

Rob No, I'm not. Look!

Rob is telling the truth. There really is
a large ferret sitting on the table.
It looks up at the boys. Suddenly
there are ferrets everywhere.

Rob Something weird is going on.
What are all these ferrets
doing here?

Lee Got it! They're the ones
who are stealing the
Vanilla Thrillers.

Rob How do you know that?

Lee   Duh … they've got the bags
in their mouths.
But the big question is –
why are they stealing
the Vanilla Thrillers?

Rob   Because they like chocolate?

Lee   Yeah, maybe. But they're not
doing this alone. My guess is
they've been trained to do it
by the Candyman. I bet he's
the evil mastermind controlling
this gang of furry felons.

Then the boys hear the sound
of a whistle. It's a signal to the ferrets.
The ferrets scamper off.

Rob   Hey, who's blowing that whistle?

Lee   The Candyman, of course.
Quick, Rob, we've got to follow
those ferrets. They'll lead us
to him.

③ Slippery Characters

The ferrets run into another part
of the factory, with the boys chasing
after them. The whistle blows again.
The ferrets climb up to an air shaft
and dive inside.

Rob   Where are those ferrets
going now?

Lee   I don't know, but they're
getting away. Move it, Rob.
Crawl inside the air shaft fast,
otherwise we'll lose them.

Rob   But that air shaft is a really
tight squeeze. I don't think I'll fit.

Lee   Of course you will. Come on,
I'll give you a push.

Rob tries to get into the shaft.
Lee gives him a shove. Rob goes in
up to his waist, but his bottom
and his legs are still sticking out.

Rob   Urrrgh. I'm stuck!

Lee	Rubbish. Just breathe in and I'll give you another shove.
Rob	It's hopeless.
Lee	No, *you're* hopeless. You can't even follow a bunch of ferrets without mucking it up.
Rob	Lee, can you stop dissing me and just pull me out?

Lee grabs hold of Rob's feet and tugs hard. Rob comes flying out like a cork from a bottle. He lands in a heap on top of Lee.

Lee   Oooooph! Rob, you want to stop eating so much toffee. No wonder you got stuck in that air shaft.

Rob   Yeah, but landing on you was like landing on a big soft marshmallow. It didn't hurt me bit!

Lee   (crossly) Whatever.

Rob   Hey, there's that whistle again.
It's coming from the alley
outside the factory.
If only we could see
who's blowing it.

Lee   We will if we can get out
into the alley fast.

Rob   How do we do that?

Lee   The same way as the ferrets –
down the air shaft.

Rob   But we can't fit in there.

Lee   Oh yes we can. Look,
there's a big tub of
the cocoa butter they use
for making chocolate.
If we jump into it, it'll make us
totally slippery. Then we'll
be able to slide down the shaft
and out into the alley!

Rob   What are we waiting for?

The boys leap into the big tub of butter.

Lee   This stuff is soooo yukky!

Rob   But it's doing the trick.
            We're as slippery as eels in oil.

Lee   Right, let's get out of this tub
            and into that air shaft!

4

The Candyman

Rob and Lee are whizzing down the airshaft.

Rob   Wow! This is better than a roller coaster.

Lee   Yeah, let's just hope we have a happy landing!

Rob   Yikes! I hadn't thought of that. Arghhhhhhh!

The boys shoot out of the air shaft
and into the alley. They land safely
on a big pile of empty cardboard boxes.

Lee   Hey, look. There's a bloke
with a whistle. He's over there
by that van.

Rob   Right. And the ferrets
are climbing into the back
of the van with the stolen bags
of Vanilla Thrillers.

Lee   Check out the name on the van.
            'Ivor Sweet-Tooth – Sweet shop
            deliveries.'

Rob   So Ivor Sweet-Tooth must be …

Lee   The Candyman!

Rob   Right! He gets the ferrets
to pinch the Vanilla Thrillers
and then he sells them
to sweet shops.

Lee   What a crook! He must
be making a fortune.
Every kid in the world wants
Vanilla Thrillers.

Rob   And so do ferrets. Look –
the Candyman's giving them
some as a reward!

Lee   So that's why ferrets
make the perfect thieves.

Rob   Yeah! Er … but how
are we going to stop them?

Lee   Let's go and get Steve.
He'll soon deal with
the Candyman!

The last ferret jumps into the back
of the van and Ivor Sweet-Tooth
shuts the doors.

Rob   Too late! The Candyman's
            getting in the van. He'll be gone
            by the time we get back here
            with Steve.

Lee   Okay, here's the plan. I'll go
and get help while you
let his tyres down.
The Candyman's van
won't be going anywhere
with four flat tyres.

Rob   But what if he sees me?

Lee   Just make like you're
an extra big ferret
and squeak at him.
He'll give you a Vanilla Thriller.

Rob   Oh no, that means
bottom burps for me!

5

What a Let-Down!

Rob lets down the van's tyres. The Candyman jumps out of the van to see what's wrong. He looks at the flat tyres and scratches his head. Then he sees Rob.

Candyman

Grrrr. I'll get you for this, you pest.

Rob   Uh-oh – time to go.

Rob runs off. The Candyman
runs after him. A big blob of cocoa butter
slides off Rob and on to the ground.
The Candyman steps on it.
He slips and slides. He's out of control.
He is skidding towards a mucky old skip.

Candyman

> Arghhhhh!

Rob   Hey, watch out
for that rubbish skip.
Whoops. Too late.

The Candyman falls head first
into the skip. He's covered
from head to toe in muck and mess!
He's really stinky! Then Steve arrives
with Lee. Steve drags the Candyman
out of the skip.

Steve   Gotcha, Mr Candyman.
Now you're coming with me
to the cop shop!

Steve marches the Candyman
off to the police station.

37

Lee   Well, I'll tell you one thing
about the Candyman.

Rob   What's that?

Lee   Even if you ate a whole bag
of Vanilla Thrillers,
your bottom burps
still wouldn't smell as bad
as he does!

About
the author

Roger Hurn has:

- been an actor in 'The Exploding Trouser Company'
- played bass guitar in a rock band
- been given the title Malam Oga (wise teacher, big boss!) while on a storytelling trip to Africa.

Now he's a writer, and he hopes you like reading about the Mystery Mob as much as he likes writing about them.

The super sweets quiz

Questions

1 Which sweets are really clever?

2 What did baby corn say to mummy corn?

3 Why don't teddy bears eat sweets?

4 Which sweet is up in space?

5 What do you call a stolen candy bar?

6 Which soft drink is the funniest?

7 What is worse than finding a maggot in your chocolate bar?

8 Why does an Aero bar go to church?

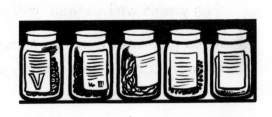

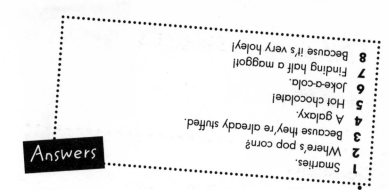

How did you score?

👋 If you got all eight super sweets answers correct, then you are smarter than a box of extra smart Smarties!

👋 If you got six super sweets answers correct, then you're well on your 'milky way'.

👋 If you got fewer than four super sweets answers correct, then you've got nothing to 'snickers' about!

When I was a kid

Question Did you eat a lot of sweets
when you were a kid?

Roger Yes. I lived in a sweet shop.

Question Wow. That must have been great!

Roger Not really. I ate too many,
so I had to go to the dentist.

Question What did the dentist say?

Roger He asked me what kind of fillings
I wanted for my teeth.

Question What did you say?

Roger I said I wanted chocolate ones.

Question Was he a good dentist?

Roger Well, he said he was painless
but he wasn't.

Question How do you know?

Roger When he stuck his finger
in my mouth, I bit him!

Adi's favourite sweet joke

Knock knock!

Who's there?

Ada!

Ada who?

Ada load of sweets and now I've got tummy ache!

Never make sweets yourself if ...

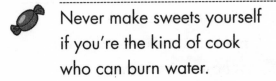

Never make sweets yourself
if you're the kind of cook
who can burn water.

*Never make sweets yourself
if the pest control company
begs you to give them your recipe.*

Never make sweets yourself
if the last time you made toast
the kitchen caught fire.

*Never make sweets yourself
if you have to look in a cookbook
to find out how to boil water.*

 Never make sweets yourself
if the smoke alarm goes off
every time you walk past the oven.

Fantastic facts about sweets

1 The first sweet was honey comb from bee hives. Cave people used to buzz off and get it.

2 The Aztec emperor Montezuma drank 50 golden goblets of hot chocolate every day. It was flavoured with chilli peppers. Now that's what I call Hot Chocolate!

3 Chocolate syrup was used for the blood in old horror movies. Yuk!

4 Never give chocolate to a dog – even a small amount can make them really ill.

5 Three out of four kids eat the ears on chocolate bunnies first.

Sweet lingo

Granulated Sugar Most sweets
are made of this (except sugar free ones).

Icing sugar A type of powdered sugar –
not a man telling his girlfriend
what he does in a rock band.

Panning A way of coating sweets
in sugar or chocolate.

Vegetable fat It's not an overweight carrot
but an oil made from vegetables
and used to make candy.

Wrapper The paper a sweet
is wrapped up in – not someone
who's into hip-hop!

Mystery Mob

Mystery Mob Set 1:

Mystery Mob and the Abominable Snowman
Mystery Mob and the Big Match
Mystery Mob and the Circus of Doom
Mystery Mob and the Creepy Castle
Mystery Mob and the Haunted Attic
Mystery Mob and the Hidden Treasure
Mystery Mob and the Magic Bottle
Mystery Mob and the Missing Millions
Mystery Mob and the Monster on the Moor
Mystery Mob and the Mummy's Curse
Mystery Mob and the Time Machine
Mystery Mob and the UFO

Mystery Mob Set 2:

Mystery Mob and the Ghost Town
Mystery Mob and the Bonfire Night Plot
Mystery Mob and the April Fools' Day Joker
Mystery Mob and the Great Pancake Race
Mystery Mob and the Scary Santa
Mystery Mob and the Conker Conspiracy
Mystery Mob and the Top Talent Contest
Mystery Mob and Midnight at the Waxworks
Mystery Mob and the Runaway Train
Mystery Mob and the Wrong Robot
Mystery Mob and the Day of the Dinosaurs
Mystery Mob and the Man Eating Tiger

RISING★STARS

Mystery Mob books are available from most booksellers.

**For mail order information
please call Rising Stars on 0871 47 23 010
or visit www.risingstars-uk.com**